HOW TO DRAW AND PAINT

CARTOONS
and Animation

HOW TO DRAW AND PAINT

CARTOONS
and Animation

PAUL JOHNSON

CHARTWELL
BOOKS, INC.

A QUARTO BOOK

Published by
Chartwell Books
A Division of Book Sales, Inc.
114 Northfield Avenue
Edison, New Jersey 08837

This edition produced for sale in the U.S.A. it's territories and dependences only

ISBN 0-7858-0040-9

This book was designed and produced by Quarto Children's Books Ltd,
The Fitzpatrick Building, 188-192 York Way, London N7 9QP

Editors Kate Burns, Samantha Hilton
Design Vivienne Gordon at Bob Gordon Design
Picture research Sarah Risley

Art Director Louise Jervis
Series design Nigel Bradley

Many people helped in the creation of this book.
Special thanks must be given to Nick Abadzis, Andy Hammond/*Garden Studio* and Nick Diggory/*Garden Studio*,
Ainsley McCloud/*The Art Collection*, Celia Canning/*Linda Rogers Associates*, Philip Norman/*Linda Rogers Associates*,
Peter Maddocks, Ross Thompson.

Typeset In House
Manufactured by Bright Arts (Pte) Ltd, Singapore
Printed in Singapore by Star Standard Industries (Pte) Ltd, Singapore

Contents

Where to start

INSTEAD OF LOOKING AT OTHER PEOPLE'S cartoons in comic books, magazines, and books, why not try to create some for yourself? Cartoons are fun to draw, and it is a challenge to think of a character, write a good story, and put it all together. This book will show you how!

▲ Greek myths
Many ancient Greeks couldn't read, so stories were told using a series of pictures. This is the same principal as comic strips today.

▲ Basic strip cartoons
Some cartoons are made into a series of pictures called a strip cartoon, which tells a story that is humorous, or serious.

EARLY CARTOONS

When the majority of the world's population was illiterate, stories and happenings were told in pictures. Many churches have stained glass windows showing biblical stories which taught people about religion. Cartoon strips today also tell a story in pictures, although the content is often more humorous than these early examples!

◄ Medieval illustrations
This german medieval picture shows a warrior about to go into battle. Pictures were very detailed and beautifully painted.

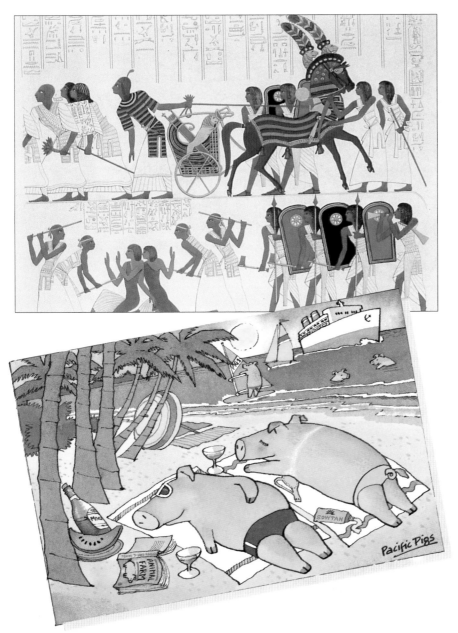

◄ Ancient Egyptian wall paintings
This copy of an ancient Egyptian wall painting shows a famous pharaoh going into battle. There are many wonderful and fantastic legends and events told by Egyptian paintings, especially on tomb walls. Even their writing, called hieroglyphs, was made from pictures and signs.

◄ Comic postcards
Comic postcards have been popular since the nineteenth century. This picture postcard shows a classic cartoon technique of showing animals behaving exactly as though they were human beings.

From pen to paper

ALL YOU NEED AT FIRST IS A PENCIL or pen and plenty of paper, to play around with ideas and develop your characters. Use rough paper to start with, as you might try out several ideas before you are ready to start on the final artwork.

EQUIPMENT

Start drawing in pencil, but not one that is too hard. Try an HB or a B, and lightly sketch out an idea. Then redraw over the lighter lines,

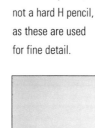

HELP! I'M A GOOD IDEA !!

Keep any ideas which look like they could be developed or adapted.

IDEAS

Use rough paper or a cheap sketchpad in the beginning.

Use a soft pencil, not a hard H pencil, as these are used for fine detail.

▼ Materials
Here are some useful materials. They include inks, watercolors, paints, felt pens, colored crayons, pens, and pastels. You probably will not need all of them, but experiment as much as possible.

▲ Pencils and crayons
Draw and color with pencils and crayons on any paper, but your picture will be neater if you use a paper with a smooth surface. When shading with crayons, try to do it in one direction only and build up the color gradually.

▼ Watercolors and inks
These are wet, so you will need a fairly thick watercolor paper to work on. Remember to do your outline with a waterproof pen or crayon, or else it will run when you start painting.

Using Different Mediums

Experiment with different types of medium and colors on various papers to see which you prefer. You may have some artist's materials, such as crayons and colored pens, at home. Or, perhaps you are able to try out others, like chunky felt pens or inks, at school. If you buy any, limit yourself to one or two of each kind, to make sure that you like using them first. There are various types of paper, some have smooth surfaces, and some have rough surfaces which soak in the colors if you use inks or felt pens on them. Keep experimenting until you feel happy with your chosen medium.

Marker pens may bleed (run), on thick paper.

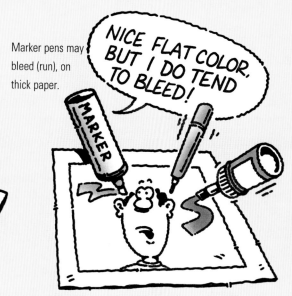

▲ Colored pens and felt pens
Draw your line with a black pen at first, then color in with chunky felt pens. It is best to work on a thin paper called "layout" paper. Chunky felt pens give a good solid, of "flat" color, and try to color in one direction, as with crayons.

► Tracing paper
Tracing paper is very useful for experimenting. You can do one drawing then put it under a sheet of tracing paper, and redraw any changes over it to make sure you like it. You can also flip (turn over) the drawing to see if it looks better the other way round.

Tracing paper with the original sketch underneath.

What style?

YOU COULD TRY TO COPY A STYLE YOU LIKE, BUT IT IS much better to develop your own way of working. That way you will be more original. The more you practice, the quicker your own style will develop.

▲ Simple black line
This line is drawn wobbly on purpose. Use pen and ink, or a thin black pen.

▲ Chunky felt pens
This simple style is good for drawing cartoons for very young children. It is drawn with marker pens.

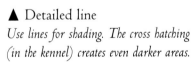

▲ Detailed line
Use lines for shading. The cross hatching (in the kennel) creates even darker areas.

▲ Pen and crayons
This combination of a pen and ink line with crayons is excellent for cartoons.

LINE WORK

You can create many varied styles with the kind of lines you draw. They can be simple or detailed; wobbly or solid. Draw lines with pencil, colored pen, or pen and ink. Use lines for shading, and cross hatching for shading darker areas. The four pictures *(left)* show how different lines and medium make very diverse effects.

SOFTER EFFECTS

Colored crayon will give a soft effect to a drawing.

This drawing shows the interesting effects of using a ball point pen.

OTHER STYLES

Study other cartoons to learn about all the different styles and mediums. Borrow ideas that you like, but try drawing them freehand, because it will help you to draw more naturally.

◄ Soft style
Use inks and watercolors for blending different shades of color, and a softer painting. These mediums work best if the paper is damp, so the colors can merge (run) into each other.

◄ Realistic styles
This style is more suited to dramatic stories, rather then funny ones. It is drawn using a fine pen line, cross hatching, and felt pens for the color.

▲ Sun
You may like the way the sun is drawn in one cartoon you see.

▲ Nose
And you may think a nose is funny in another cartoon.

▲ Whole picture
So why not put these two things together in one picture yourself?

15

What to draw?

YOU COULD SIT AND STARE AT A BLANK piece of paper waiting for inspiration, but it may never arrive! Instead, look around you, wherever you are – at home, at school, on a bus, or at the zoo. Your cartoon character can be based on a person, an animal, even an inanimate object, or it could be totally from your imagination.

BABIES

Some people are naturally funny. Babies are great to draw. Their big heads on little bodies already make them look like a cartoon. Practice drawing them both in real life and from a photograph, and in various positions – sitting, crawling, or tottering about.

PETS

Pets make very good cartoon characters, and they will not complain about the likeness! Try sketching them from life, but if they keep moving or it is too difficult, draw them from photographs or magazines.

FAMILIES

Draw the people in your family doing everyday things, such as cooking or watching television. Before long, you could have drawn a cartoon family.

▲ Photographic reference
Use photographs you have of your family, friends, and pets to study different positions, faces, expressions, and characteristics.

16

▲ Studying people
Study strangers as well as friends. Each person has a unique characteristic or manner which can be turned into part of a cartoon.

RESEARCH

It is very useful if you can always carry a sketchpad with you in case you see a face or a character that could be adapted into a cartoon. You will find things that can be part of your cartoon in everyday life, or if you go on a special trip. The zoo is a great place to study and draw a wide range of animals, which you would normally only see in books or on the television.

▲ Studying animals
At the zoo you can study how the animals look, as well as the way they move, wash, and eat.

▼ Media
Look carefully at people and creatures on the television, and keep newspaper cuttings in a scrapbook of anything interesting.

Body forms

I N MOST CARTOONS ONE OR TWO FEATURES of the body are usually exaggerated. This creates the humor of the drawing. If you learn to draw normal human bodies first, you can then experiment with cartoon versions – perhaps drawing very fat, thin, tall, or short bodies.

HOW TO DRAW

A good basic way to start drawing people is to make a simple figure first, and gradually add on more detailed features and clothes to give your person a unique character.

◄ Stick figures
You can start by drawing a stick figure, and then drawing round it to give it clothes, hands, and feet. Also, try drawing it in different positions such as walking or sitting. Keep it simple.

◄ Ovals and circles
Another way is to draw the body as a series of ovals and circles. Where the ovals join are the joints of the body. You can then experiment with fatter or thinner ovals to create different body shapes and characteristics.

LOOKING AT PEOPLE

Look carefully at your subject, and just draw what you see. It does not matter if it's not a masterpiece, or if you get some things wrong. Mistakes can sometimes be useful or funny. It is best to draw from life, but if you need a difficult position you can use photographs. But try to avoid tracing the body, as this will not help you to understand its shape.

◀ From photo to sketchpad
It can be useful to look at a photograph to study a person's dominant characteristics closely. Use these to create a cartoon figure in your sketchpad.

PEOPLE SHAPES

Heads stay almost the same size, but the height of the body changes with age. Cartoon characters often have small bodies and big heads as the face is very important.

▼ Cross section
Draw a whole age range of people from a baby to an old person. This is a good way to examine how the body changes with age.

19

Big head!

T HE HEAD IS THE MOST IMPORTANT feature on a cartoon person, so it is worth learning how to draw it well. Once you have mastered the basic shape, it is easy to add on different features, such as hairstyles, beards, and glasses. You can then try drawing a side- or back-view of a head.

▲ Shapes
A real head is not round like a football, but slightly oval in shape.

HEADS AND NECKS

Give a thin person a neck, and a slightly longer oval shaped head. But a fat head sits right on the shoulders, and is a rounder and fatter oval shape. Experiment with the shape of the head until you are happy with it, as it will be such an important feature in your cartoon.

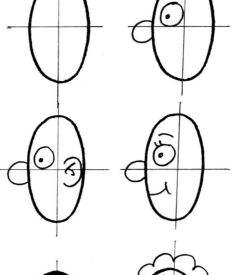

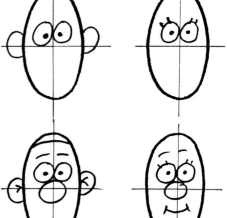

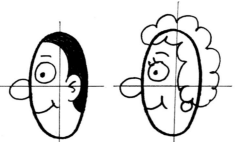

▶ **Proportions**
This is a good way to draw a correct head. The eyes go just above the centerline.

▶ **Adding features**
This is the correct place to put in the nose and mouth.

▶ **Hair**
Add the eyebrows, eyelashes, and the hair last. The hair is also an important feature.

Some people have very big chins on long, thin faces.

Reverse the long, thin face to create the opposite effect.

Some heads are long and thin but egg shaped.

Beards and mustaches can be added to your basic head shape.

ADDING FEATURES

You can add on extra features to your basic head and face. Everything goes toward creating expression and character. Think about different hairstyles, noses, mouths, and eyes. Glasses can be used with different characters, from old people, to fierce teachers, to mad scientists.

Beards can be big and bushy, drawn with an outline and colored in. Mustaches can be a few lines, or large and curly.

BASIC DETAILS

Cartoon eyes, noses, and mouths are usually big to allow more room for exaggerated expression. Eyes can be sleepy, weepy, or scared, and mouths can be happy, sad, or surprised.

HAIRSTYLES

Hair can be drawn as a scribble, a solid black line, or as an outline to be filled in with color. Useful tips are that babies have very little hair, and old men tend to go bald.

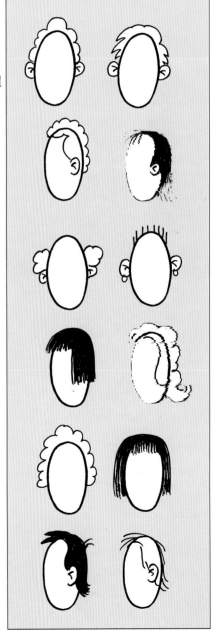

Cartoon creatures

IF YOU WANT TO MAKE A CARTOON creature, first practice how to draw the real thing. This will help you to understand its individual characteristics. Once you know an animal well, it is much easier to play around with a sketch of it and work out what you would like to emphasize. Some animals are naturally funny, and baby animals are especially good if you want a cute character.

WHICH ANIMAL TO CHOOSE?

You can choose any animal you like, and they need not be real. Dinosaurs are fun to draw, because they are extinct you can be very imaginative! This spread looks at all the different features of animals that you can put in your cartoon.

you're shocking!

Some animals are furry. It is a good technique to exaggerate this.

Huge animals make excellent cartoon subjects.

Some creatures are scaly and spikey, which can make them fierce or funny.

 And so do tiny ones. You can use insects as well as animals.

▲ Funny animals
Some animals are naturally funny. Here are a few examples — ostriches, pigs, tree frogs, ardvaarks, crocodiles, and toucans. Just pick the feature you think is the funniest and really exaggerate it in your drawing. If an animal is not odd looking, then you might have to emphasize more than one characteristic.

RESEARCH

Try to avoid animals which have been made into cartoons many times, unless you can think of a new way to draw them. There are plenty of ways of finding amusing or interesting animals. The zoo will have unusual ones, and parks or farms will have many animals that you can sketch.

USING PICTURES

You can always just copy animals and ideas from books, magazines and the television. Or, even look at paintings in art galleries.

ANIMAL FEATURES

Particular animals will have their own obvious features, and it is these you need to study well so you can exaggerate them in your cartoon. Here are some obvious examples, but keep an eye out all the time for new and funny ideas.

Give dogs wet noses, wagging tails, and floppy or pricked up ears.

Pigs need big snouts, curly tails and ears that flop about.

This duck has an extra large beak.

▶ Feet
It is easy to forget the importance of feet, but they are funny and varied, and can be full of character. Birds and monsters have scaly skin and sharp claws; ducks have webbed feet; and elephants have enormous toenails!

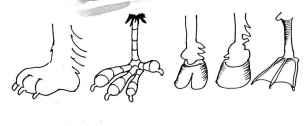

Animal antics

Y OU CAN CHOOSE JUST ONE CREATURE to make into a cartoon, but it would get a bit lonely! So add a friend, or even an enemy. Or maybe you could create a whole cartoon jungle, a woodland scene, or an undersea world. You can also use your imagination to make your own animals up.

WHAT TO CHANGE?

It is up to you how much you change an animal into a cartoon. Do you make four legged animals stand up and walk? Do you give them clothes to wear, or alter their natural colors? The only rule is to take care that their special features, such as a tiger's stripes or a rabbit's ears, remain recognizable.

1 *One way to draw a cartoon creature is to sketch out a rough, simple shape first of all.*

2 *Add the animal's special, main features. Dogs need predominant noses, eyes and ears, and a tail to wag.*

3 *Make your animal happy with a big smile, like this dog, or sad with a downturned mouth.*

4 *Now fill in the details to make your cartoon character complete. This dog has a shiny, wet nose, bright eyes, and a panting tongue.*

Draw a real hare first. Keep its big ears, teeth, and tail as you change it.

It stands up and its paws become hands.

Dress it as you want, but keep its big ears and buck teeth.

Make a hare's attributes, such as speed, a funny part of the cartoon.

▲ Manic panic
A huge grin, big round eyes, and copious amounts of wild fur make this cat look manic, even though its shape is very basic and can be drawn easily.

ANIMAL CHARACTERISTICS

As you work think about the sort of character you want your creature to have. Is it to be clever, or maybe a bit dumb? Will it have a special attribute, such as speed or strength? The face is an important place to create character, and some creatures already look naturally wicked, clever or dumb. But there are lots of things you can do. Sometimes you will need to keep its real color to help keep its identity – a bat must be black to be spooky. With most four-legged creatures, it's possible to make them stand on their hind legs, and use their front paws as hands. And with birds, you can adapt the feathers on the wings to look like arms and hands, or get rid of the wings altogether and draw arms instead. Think about whether it wears clothes, and if so, what kind?

► Dumb or bright?
This cartoon dog is a blood hound. This type of dog looks dumb anyway, but its features have been exaggerated to give it slow, sleepy eyes and a lumbering shape. In contrast, the bird is quick-witted, and quick-limbed. Its glasses and book are clear, recognizable reflections of a clever character.

► Wild and wicked
Vultures are usually depicted as wicked and sly in cartoons. Note the angry eyes and pointing finger. The crocodile's big teeth are its main feature.

Anything goes

CARTOONS ARE ABLE TO BREATHE LIFE into anything. Unlike photographs or live action movies, any object will come to life given a face, a pair of hands, and a pair of legs. The face is where you can show its personality most easily, as a mouth or eyes will make any object happy or sad, tired or worried.

▼ Magic pencils!
With your pencil and some imagination you can magic anything into life!

BRING IT TO LIFE

For inspiration on which objects to bring to life look all around you — in your bedroom, kitchen, school, or yard. Types of plants make good cartoons, especially vegetables. You could turn your house into a character, with windows for eyes and a door for the mouth, and create a cartoon family to live in it.

Think how a saucepan would feel if it were alive.

Would a tea cup feel proud or annoyed to be filled with hot tea?

Do pedal bikes secretly yearn to be the speed kings of the road?

As if by magic!

ONCE YOU HAVE AN IDEA DRAW lots of doodles on rough paper. Try to emphasize one particular feature of your object. If you bring a brick to life, make it look heavy; if you choose a balloon, it must look light. Try shapes that are fairly simple to draw, because the fewer the unimportant details the better.

CARS

Cars are good to draw because there are so many types and you can have fun with their personalities. Draw friendly, little cars with rounded lines and a smiling bumper; or fast, aggressive cars with a long radiator for a mouth and wicked eyes instead of the headlights.

Other ideas
Trains, planes, boats, and tankers are also popular. Think up something to make your character different, such as a boat that doesn't like water, or an airplane that is scared of heights.

28

A FAMILY OF OBJECTS

Perhaps you may decide to have a number of objects
all living in one place, such as cups and saucers,
teapots, and knives and forks whose home is the
kitchen. Think what their personalities may be – is the
china delicate, are the pots and pans tough? Do they
all like each other, or are there certain characters who
are always arguing or sulking with each other?

◀ Personalize objects
*Cutlery is easy to give a
personality to, as they already
have "bodies" and "hairstyles."
Just add a face, and maybe
arms and legs, and they
come alive.*

▶ Main characters
*You could have a main object
character, such as "Teapot
Tim," or "Sally Sugar." Learn
to draw it well from all
different angles. Draw it so
often that it becomes a friend.
It is common in cartoons to
have an object, which although
secondary to an animate
character, is still the leader of
the inanimate object gang.*

29

Fantasy characters

IF YOU HAVE A VIVID IMAGINATION your cartoon character can come entirely from your mind. Fantasy subjects are ideal for cartoons and animation. You can escape from the real world and invent what you like — as long as you can draw it! Fantasy creatures can live in a completely made-up world, in outer space, or even inside the human body.

▲ Wonderman!
This realistic, superhero style is good for dramatic action-packed stories.

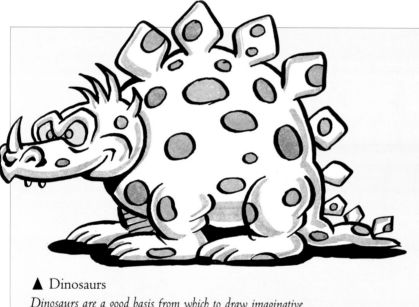

▲ Dinosaurs
Dinosaurs are a good basis from which to draw imaginative ones. You can mix up various types to create your own.

STRANGE SHAPES

Fantastic fantasy characters and monsters can be humorous or serious. Space creatures, for instance, can be funny shapes and colors, or hard and menacing with angular lines and metallic colors.

This "enemy" space creature is drawn to look aggressive.

Ghosts are soft and loose and can be any shape you want.

Robots are the opposite to ghosts, with strong colors and clear lines.

SILHOUETTES

Use black ink to paint silhouettes, which are good for spooky ghosts, shadows, and bats.

Mix animals to create a fantasy friend, or foe.

Sharp teeth, and fierce eyes make this silly creature scary.

CHARACTERS NEED STORIES

There are no limits to what you can draw, but whether it is funny or action-packed, you still need a good storyline. You could invent the most wonderful fantasy characters ever seen, but they are lifeless until there is a plot. So as well as what they look like, think about what they will do, and how they will do it.

1 *Your super-character will begin life brimming with action and enthusiasm.*

2 *But with no plot or enemies to conquer, his powers will soon start to fade away.*

3 *So now is the time to create a story for your character — or he will soon fall fast asleep.*

Fairytale foes

THE CLASSIC CARTOON SCENARIO involves a battle between two different characters. They can be good or evil, strong, or weak, clever or stupid. Many cartoon characters have been inspired by ancient myths, fairytales, and legends. There are innocent types such as pixies, elves, and gnomes; and more sinister ones such as ghosts, vampires, witches, and wizards.

DUHH!

Scientists are good or evil – fighting to either save or destroy the world.

IMAGINATION

It is easy to show who is good, and who is bad. Draw evil characters with dark colors, black clothes, downturned mouths, and pointed noses. Good characters can be drawn with soft lines, and pale or bright colors. Some characters can be good or bad, such as skeletons or ghosts, depending on their facial expressions. But the good guys will always need an enemy with whom to fight, and vice versa.

Vampires wear black, with blood-stained fangs, and often have a bat nearby.

Fairies are usually good, but also mischievous.

32

MYTHICAL FIGURES

You will find many good ideas in books on myths and legends that are full of strange creatures, such as centaurs, mermaids, and giants. Many myths have monsters which are half-animal, half-human, especially the Greek Myths. You can make up your own strange and wonderful combinations.

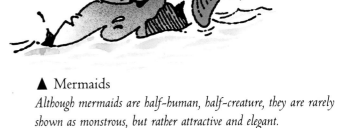

▲ Mermaids
Although mermaids are half-human, half-creature, they are rarely shown as monstrous, but rather attractive and elegant.

▲ Witches
Draw wicked witches with pointed noses and chins, tall hats, and dark clothes. They are often accompanied by a black cat called a "familiar."

▶ Giants
Giants are a popular fairytale figure, so you can find lots of visual references for them. This drawing uses perspective to make the giant look very tall (see pp. 50-51). Giants can be gentle or blood-thirsty.

Giving it life

THINK ABOUT HOW THE CHARACTER WILL ACT, AS IF IT WERE A real person. What will make it different or special? Write a list of things it can or can't do, and start to draw pictures of it from different angles. In this way you will build up a character sheet that you can refer to while you draw.

CREATING YOUR CHARACTER

Your character sheet could look something like this (below). Use it to remind you of the way your character looks and acts, otherwise you can discover that it looks different at the end of your cartoon strip than at the start. Give your character a catchy name.

► Hands

Hands can express a lot about your cartoon character, and even cartoon hands need plenty of drawing practice. If your character is a superhero, he will need realistic hands, but others can be very simple. Often cartoonists draw hands with just a thumb and three fingers.

► Feet

Feet and footwear are as important a part of human cartoon characters as animal ones. Barefeet can be very varied, and are often funny. Feet also show the way a person walks, runs, or stands. And different types of shoes indicate a great deal about the character's age, taste, and profession.

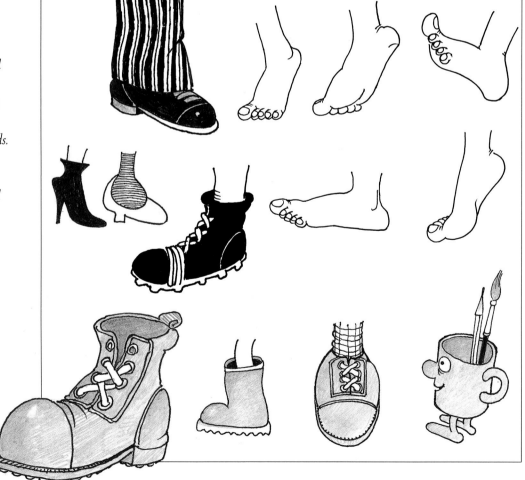

35

Expressive faces

YOUR CARTOON FACE NEEDS TO BE able to show the whole range of human emotions. But you must be able to do this with the minimum of drawing, so that the particular emotion you want to convey is really obvious. You will notice that most expressions are shown with the mouth and eyes.

Faces show the whole spectrum of human feelings.

◀ Different styles
Different styles make different characters. The three boxes (below) show, firstly, a really simple cartoon style, suitable for a short joke; the next shows a more detailed character, which you could develop farther; the last realistic style is good for an action comic strip with a serious, dramatic content. In the end, you should decide what style and level you feel confident with, and work from there.

 +  +  =

1 *Experiment with a face by drawing a blank, or nearly blank, head to start.*

2 *Add on different hairstyles drawn on tracing paper placed over the original.*

3 *Try drawing a mustache, or any other feature, on another sheet of tracing paper.*

4 *Complete the picture with a beard on a third tracing paper layer.*

FACIAL FEATURES

All human beings have the same basic features, so their individuality depends on how you draw them. There are standard ways of drawing different emotions. Scared people's hair stands on end; surprise is shown by raised eyebrows, and sleepy people have half-closed eyes. Make faces at yourself in the mirrror to study different expressions.

▼ Noses
Cartoon noses are generally exaggerated to make the face funnier. They can be made longer, bigger, or into a button shape for babies.

▼ Hair
Many well-known cartoon characters have distinctive hairstyles. Hair can make your character look scruffy, glamorous, young, or old.

▼ Eyes
Eyes can be simple black dots; more expressive eyes are dots in white circles, or semi-circles, with eyebrows.

▼ Mouths
The simplest mouth is just a line and a solid black shape when it opens. A mouth can have teeth, shown as a block or as individual teeth.

On the move

NOW YOU HAVE CREATED your ideal character, and given it a name and an identity, you need to make it have adventures, or get into tricky situations. And for this you need to make it move.

▲ Oops!
Getting flattened by a heavy weight and becoming paper-thin is a classic cartoon joke.

MOVEMENT

When someone walks they have one or both feet on the ground. But when they run draw both feet off the ground to help give the impression of speed.

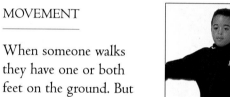

Your character can stroll along (left), or really whizz along (below).

▲ Fish lady!
Your character can grow an extra feature, such as wings or fins to enable it to swim or fly as part of the story.

▲ Watch out!
Cartoon characters "tread water" in mid-air before they fall off cliffs. Draw speed marks to show fast movement.

WHAT CAN YOUR CHARACTER DO?

The wonderful thing about cartoons is that you can make your character do absolutely anything, as long as you are able to draw it!

Much cartoon humor is "slapstick" and involves such things as cliffs, danger signs, or ten-ton weights. Violence has always been an element in cartoons. It is not the real world, so characters get squashed, dropped, or blown up and still survive.

YOUR CARTOON CHARACTER CAN DO ANYTHING!

Your character can fly to outerspace, and all sorts of other exciting and dangerous acts!

▶ Action
Your character can go anywhere, even catch a rocket to the moon. Since it is not the real world, anything is believable.

Your character can grow tiny or bigger than the world itself.

A huge bump on the head is a classic bit of "slapstick" humor.

39

Human oddballs

LOOK AROUND YOU AT THE ENDLESS variety of people. They are all possible subjects! Your comic strip could become really boring if all the people in it looked the same, so here are a selection of other types who could also feature.

Good little children have neat clothes and hair.

Naughty kids have scruffy clothes and hair, and a wicked grin!

CHILDREN

All your cartoon children should have different personalities. Some may never do anything wrong, and be little angels. And others may be just the opposite, always getting into trouble, playing practical jokes and pranks. Maybe they are smart, or very streetwise?

Babies have big heads, little wobbly bodies, and huge mouths!

◀ Foreigners
Here are some stereotypes of different races. They may be useful as "extras" in your cartoons, or you can develop them farther if you want.

HISTORY

You can also do an historical cartoon strip. Lots of characters from history are fun to draw, and their costumes make them instantly recognizable. Try Vikings, Romans, cavemen, or Native Americans, for instance.

▼ Comic references

Look through comic books and newspapers to find lots of stereotypes of different ages, characters, and people's dress-sense. Do not copy them exactly, but use them to give you ideas for extra people, like parents or relatives, in your cartoon.

Crazy work

Some of the characters in your cartoon strip could have jobs. The storyline could then include things to do with going to work or problems involved in their jobs. Perhaps a chef who can't cook, or a scientist whose experiments never work or have odd results. The character can be bungling or brilliant at the job — but bungling is funnier!

CARTOON JOBS

Schoolteachers often feature in cartoons. You could base one on a teacher that you know — but don't be too unkind! The picture (below) shows good ideas on what to include when you draw a teacher.

▼ Other professions
Some jobs are naturally funny, or outrageous, like this pop star. You could give your character a job that you would really love to have, or one that you think would be really boring — your character could think so too!

ACCESSORIES

Give your character
items to carry or wear
which help make the job
really obvious.

Soldiers should
look <u>unlike</u> the
ideal recruit.

▶ Attention!
*Real soldiers are supposed to be fit and
alert, so to create funny ones make
them look bored and unfit. Give them
big boots and oversized helmets which
almost cover their eyes.*

THE ARTS

Artists are easy to draw as they wear
paint smeared smocks and berets,
and will always have a palette and
paint brush in their hands.

TRANSFORMATION

The character could be an
ordinary working person by day,
but at night, an amazing
transformation takes place to
create someone larger than life!

1 *To make a strong contrast your
ordinary person must be very normal,
or boring and weak looking. You could
use dull colors to emphasize this point.*

2 *You need a special way in which the
transformation takes place. Maybe
while running, spinning around, or in a
phone box — anywhere you want!*

3 *The superhero, or heroine, needs to look
very strong and dynamic. Perhaps with
a brightly colored special outfit, and bulging
muscles to help their battle against evil.*

Cool creatures

REAL ANIMALS DON'T SHOW FACIAL expressions in the same way that humans do. You can't tell if a bird or frog is happy or sad by its face. But once animals become cartoon characters they need to be able to show all the same emotions as humans, otherwise they will have no personality.

◀ Ducks
A real duck bill is very rigid, but a cartoon one is flexible to show different expressions.

▼ Animal babies
Animal babies are good for showing really cute, or slightly pathetic, emotions.

These puppy dogs (below) show how to draw an animal changing from happy to unsure, to exhausted and unhappy. Note the steadily drooping tails and ears, and the drops of sweat (or tears) on the last puppy.

1,2,3,4. 1,2,3,4. Wag youR tails children!

EXPRESSIONS

A cartoon creature's feelings — just like a cartoon human's — are centered in the mouth (or beak), and the eyes. So these particular features should be drawn and made to move in an exaggerated way.

For example, cartoon frogs could have very wide mouths which are long and thin when shut, but can open to talk, or laugh, just like a human being, and you can give them a human-looking tongue. Bears have button eyes, and smiling mouths (right), which make them look friendly, but just add teeth and they become fierce. Look at the other ideas on these pages for good ways to draw expressive faces on a variety of creatures.

◀ Monkeys
Monkeys have very wide mouths which go right across their faces. Their mouths can stretch and twist into all sorts of strange expressions. Their eyes are positioned high up on their heads.

◀ Dogs
Dogs can have very expressive ears as well as faces. A cartoon dog will smile and prick up its ears when it is happy. But when it is sad its mouth and ears will droop right down. Draw dots instead of whiskers.

▼ Cats
Draw cats' emotions in the same way as dogs, but note that they also have big whiskers that reflect a feline's mood.

▼ Insects
Greatly exaggerate insects' eyes and mouths, so that they have enough room to have expressions like any other creature.

Wiggles and waddles

ANIMALS MOVE IN SUCH A VARIETY of ways, all of them very different from humans. You may have decided to make your animal character walk on two legs, but even then creatures walk differently – a penguin waddles, a snake slithers, and a kangaroo hops.

HOW DIFFERENT CREATURES MOVE

The way a creature is drawn moving can add a great deal to its character – and understanding this movement will help when it comes to animation later on in the book. Some creatures, such as snakes or fish, can't walk anyway – or can they? On the other hand you may have created a pig that flies or an elephant that rides a scooter!

▼ Jumping
Frogs and kangaroos jump very high, but in different ways. Frogs stretch right out, but kangaroos bounce up and down.

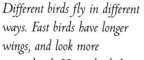
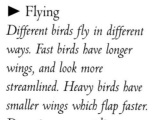

▶ Flying
Different birds fly in different ways. Fast birds have longer wings, and look more streamlined. Heavy birds have smaller wings which flap faster. Draw in movement lines.

CHARACTERISTIC MOVEMENT

Animals running on all fours stretch out their legs, then pull them all in together (except horses that use alternate legs). Four-legged animals running on two legs use their front limbs as arms. Birds with long legs walk slowly and pick their feet up, while chickens and ducks scrape and waddle.

► Monkeys
Monkeys swing hanging from one arm or their tail. Draw their arms much longer than their legs.

◄ Mice
Follow the rule that when a mouse runs on either four or two legs, all their legs are off the ground. If they are on their hind legs, use their front legs as arms in a human running position.

◄ Penguins
Penguins cannot fly, so they have small wings but big feet. They waddle and slip over on the ice, which can look very funny.

◄ Fish
Fish bend their tails to swim. Or you can make one walk with tail fins as feet.

EEK!

BIG BRICK WALL.

Basic backgrounds

Once you've designed them, your characters will need scenes to be in, whether it's a real or a fantasy world. The scene, or background, can help in all sorts of ways. It makes the cartoon more interesting, and shows if it's set in contemporary or historical time, and where the action is taking place — in a city, the country, or outer-space.

SCENERY

As you plan a scene, think about whether it is indoor or outdoor, and how your character will be placed in it — in the foreground or a speck?

◀ **Scenery behind?**
Your character is <u>in</u> the scene, so the scenery need not always be behind the character.

◀ **Detail**
An indoor scene could have just a door and a window, but most rooms have all sorts of things in them.

BASIC BACKGROUNDS

Think of the different places you have been to, maybe on vacation, or even scenes you have seen in magazines or on television. But keep the scene fairly simple, so that it is really obvious what kind of background view it is.

▼ **A River**
A simple cartoon river is painted blue with paler colored ripples on it.

▼ **A Beach**
Keep the sea simple, and don't do too many waves. The sand should be a speckled yellow.

SCENERY RESEARCH

When you plan a general background scene think of where your characters will be positioned in it. Don't make the scene so cluttered that there is no space for them. And you can try to make the actual scenery humorous or dramatic to suit the story.

In a space scene do the sky a dark color, and the rest in unusual colors.

Position your characters carefully in the scenery.

▼ A Park

Draw a park bench with railings, simple trees, and some pigeons.

▼ A Staircase

Indoor views are drawn with fairly straight lines.

▼ A Rough Sea

Draw sharp pointed waves. If you add a boat, do it at a dramatic sharp tilt.

Perspective is easy!

EVEN THOUGH YOUR DRAWING IS A flat picture on flat paper, you can create an illusion of depth and distance by using perspective. This will enable you to draw objects from any angle.

▼ Distance

Perspective is the way to show distance in your drawings. To understand perspective, look down a highway or railroad. As the lines of the railroad (below) or highway (right) go farther away from you, they seem to get smaller until they disappear at a "vanishing point."

The near cactus looks bigger than the distant one.

The distant sleepers look smaller.

▲ Vanishing point
The girl in the picture (above) is pointing to the "vanishing point" where the road disappears on the horizon level.

Perspective Anywhere

Perspective works in any direction that you look. So, if you look up, near things are big and far things are small, and it will be the same if you look down.

    The angle of perspective you use may influence the shape of the frame (see pp. 64-65) you create for your cartoon. You can create really dramatic scenes if you use perspective in an interesting way, but even using it a little will make your picture look less flat.

Look down a tall building. The cars are tiny, and the building narrows toward the sidewalk.

Look up a tall building and the top looks narrower, and the clouds and airplanes are small.

Dramatic shots

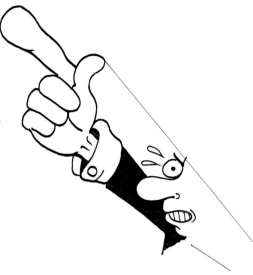

 ONCE YOU GET THE HANG OF SIMPLE perspective you can try out some really unusual angles. They may not look right at first, but keep practicing. Sometimes they can really add to the excitement of a cartoon strip.

CHARACTER PERSPECTIVE

Perspective not only works on backgrounds, but can also be used to draw the characters themselves. It's a little harder as there are less straight lines, but it can create dynamic action pictures. Perspective can be useful to show the difference between large and small characters in the same cartoon frame (left and below).

The dinosaur is drawn in perspective. Its great height is shown by the difference in size between its feet and head. Perspective emphasizes the fact that the dinosauris standing behind the child in the foreground.

◀ Bird's eye view

Imagine that a bird is looking down on the flying boy. It would see a person with a big head, and a body that narrows down to small feet. The effect is even more pronounced by the huge hand right in the foreground of the picture, and the relatively small buildings down below.

◀ Worm's eye view

In contrast, imagine that a worm is just out of sight at the bottom of the picture and is looking up at the boy. It would see enormous feet, and a body narrowing to a small head. Also note that the trees get narrower toward the sky. This all helps to create a very dramatic picture in which character perspective and background perspective work well together.

Moody scenes

MAKING A STRIP CARTOON IS LIKE making a movie. You need a good storyline, a superstar (your character), the right setting (your backgrounds), different camera angles (the perspective), and finally the lighting and dramatic effects department to enhance the atmosphere!

DAY SCENES

To create different atmospheres in day scenes you can draw or paint different types of skies.

These suns range from very hot (left), to a setting sun (middle), to a bright day sun (right).

NIGHT SCENES

Night scenes help to show the passage of time, and to create a spooky atmosphere. Show warm-colored lights shining from a dark building, and the moon and stars.

▼ Calm, sunny day
This is shown by blue skies and clouds that look like cotton wool balls.

▼ Cloudy
The sky is filling up with less friendly looking clouds.

▲ Storms approaching
Storm clouds are large, dark, and ominous and take up most the of sky.

▲ Sunsets and sunrises
The sun is low on the horizon, and the sky is pink and orange.

WEATHER

Weather can change a scene dramatically, and it is quite easy to draw. Try snow or rain (below) or flashes of lightning.

I WISH HE WOULDN'T KEEP DRAWING ALL THIS RAIN !

JUST BECAUSE IT'S EASY !

I WISH HE WOULDN'T KEEP DRAWING ALL THIS SNOW !

JUST BECAUSE IT'S EASY !

SHADOWS

Putting shadows in pictures adds to the realism. Although real shadows are blue/black in tone, cartoon ones are effective as solid black.

A sun high in the sky makes short shadows.

A sun low in the sky makes long shadows.

Forefront light puts the background in shadow.

Background light puts the forefront in shadow.

ALTERNATIVE METHODS

Scary scenes will create the right kind of atmosphere if your character is frightened – like this man below!

Get in shape!

YOU HAVE NOW DESIGNED your cartoon characters and worked out how to do backgrounds and special effects. Your next step is to put them together to make a series of interesting and clever scenes. Experiment with different ways until you find the most effective.

▲ Dream worlds
Use a wiggly frame to create a dream bubble shape. This makes it obvious that the character is dreaming he is flying, rather than actually flying.

◄ Split frames
This technique is also used on the television or in the movies, at it is a very clear way to show two people in different places talking to each other on the telephone.

▲ Through the keyhole
Frame a character or an object as though someone is looking through a keyhole. A pair of binoculars is also very effective.

◄ Caught in the act
Highlighting a character in a shaft of light, such as torchlight, or under a street lamp, will create a dramatic composition.

SPECIAL EFFECTS

This spread looks at a variety of ways to make your pictures have a genuine impact. One way is by putting different frames round your pictures (see pp. 64-65); another method is to vary the size and shape of images within the frame.

▼ Size creates impact
Using silhouettes against a huge sun or moon will liven up potentially uninteresting scenes. Also, simple scenes like these (below) can make an effective gap between two busy scenes.

◄ Zoom in and out
Just as a movie camera zooms in and out on different scenes, so you can by changing the space filled by your character.

◄ Change the shape
You can have wide scenes (or tall ones). Wide scenes are great for vast, lonely expanses like seas or deserts.

Titles and type

IT IS BEST TO GIVE A STRIP cartoon a title, especially if you intend to do more than one. It's a good idea to have the name of your main character in the title, or just have its name as the title, so it's easily remembered. "Terry Dactyl" sounds more catchy than, "The Adventures of Terry Dactyl," and it is a lot less hard work to hand letter each time.

TITLE LETTERING

Title lettering is very important as it will be the first thing that people look at in the cartoon strip. You can create a variety of styles, which match the content of the cartoon. For funny cartoons, don't make your lettering look too serious, and hand draw them, rather than use a ruler. If your cartoon is full of action and adventure, make your lettering look dramatic; if your character wears a stripy shirt, make your title stripy too.

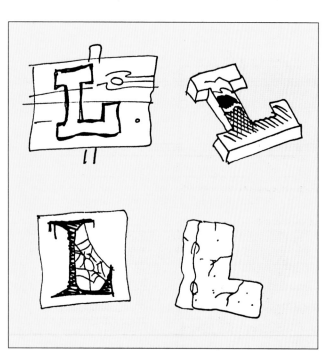

◄ Type styles
These letters show a wild west, a stone age, a horror story, and a futuristic style. Or you could do letters shaped like bubbles, or decorated with patterns, or chunky with drop shadows.

▼ Logos
The title lettering can incorporate the main character, and this becomes a "logo." Put this at the start of your cartoon.

BUT I DISTINCTLY HEARD YOU SAY 'WAITER'!

◀ Simple captions

For simple, single cartoons you can just have the "punchline," as a caption rather than combining the text and the picture.

This style is very simple and effective, and it is often used in cartoons in newspapers.

◀ Expressive words

You can use letters to express feelings, either emotional or physical. This picture shows, in a humorous fashion, the confusion of the detective, the anger of the person on the other end of the telephone, and the mood of the girl — all without any proper words.

WORDS OR NOT ?

Some cartoons are so obvious that they don't need any captions or type, especially the humorous black and white type; they may not even need a title. This allows them to be understood by people from any country.

▼ Pictures that tell a story

This picture tells the story with no words at all. You can do a whole strip without words, but the pictures must be clear and simple.

Crash, bang! Ouch!

THERE ARE MANY DIFFERENT ways to add humorous effects to your pictures. Some are a means of showing sound, while others perhaps indicate movement, show pain, or special lighting effects. You may be able to invent some of your own, and they all help to make the cartoon strip look more visual and fun. Try to imagine new sound effects and then right them down – Kerplunk!

PICTORIAL SOUND EFFECTS

Some sound effects do not need words to be clear. If someone is hit on the head they will see stars, and their head will "spin" around and around (see above). Explosions are fun to draw with clouds of smoke, whirls, and exclamation marks. A bright idea is usually shown by a light bulb above the head.

◀▼ Action lines
These lines show objects and characters performing an action. Make the lines suit the picture: this bell (see below) has wavy "sound" lines, and the spilt drink (see left) looks like drops of liquid.

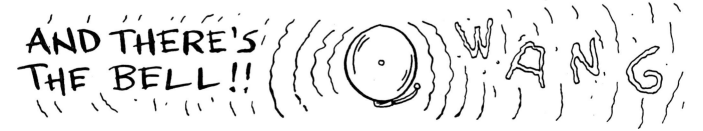

AND THERE'S THE BELL!! WANG

SHOWING MOVEMENT

Fast movement is easy to draw. Draw speed lines coming from the moving object. Draw each line as a single stroke which gradually fades off. Make the object lean forward as well, and you can draw clouds of steam or smoke coming from it.

EXPRESSIVE WORDS

Both animals and humans can talk in cartoons. Animals can also make proper noises, such as "eek" for a mouse, and "miaow" for a cat. Words can also describe sound effects, such as "Boom" or "Crunch". If it is a loud or sudden sound effect you can draw in an exclamation mark, or two.

Bubbles and boxes

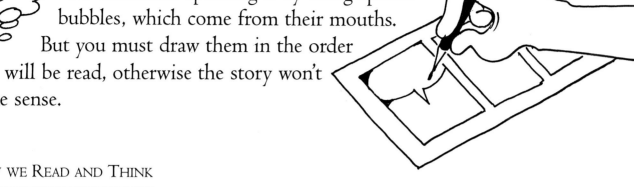

THE EASIEST WAY TO SHOW CARTOON characters speaking is by using speech bubbles, which come from their mouths. But you must draw them in the order they will be read, otherwise the story won't make sense.

HOW WE READ AND THINK

If your character has a lot to say, a big bubble will be needed, so make sure you have room for it without covering too much of the picture.

▲ Reading order

Read the question first, then the answer. Not all words need to be in bubbles, especially if they are more like sound effects, but make sure you leave a clear space in which to draw them.

▲ Thought bubbles

Thought bubbles are drawn like smoke clouds. They come from the brain, not the mouth, and are drawn slightly differently to speech bubbles.

Speech Bubbles

It is important to keep your story short, clear, and simple. Any words you need apart from speech can be put into boxes at the top and bottom of the picture. Bubbles are usually oval in shape. Keep them white with black lettering. Bubbles can also contain other sounds apart from words, such as loud music or singing.

I AM VERY VERY ANGRY!!

A hard, jagged outline immediately tells you that the person speaking is either angry or talking very loudly.

A DROPPED CAPITAL CAN LOOK ATTRACTIVE...

Use capital letters. They are neater and easier to read.

TWO PEOPLE MAY SAY THE SAME THING.

Two people can say the same thing if you join them both to the same bubble.

... AND A COMBINATION OF LIGHT AND **BOLD** LETTERS MAKES MORE **INTERESTING** READING ...

Bold letters and an underline will emphasize an important word.

USE JAGGED BUBBLES FOR WORDS THAT COME FROM RADIOS OR TELEPHONES OR THE T.V. OR ROBOTS!!

Use jagged bubbles for words that come from machines, like radios or robots.

The frame

BY NOW YOU SHOULD KNOW ALL YOU need to create great cartoon pictures, but each picture will usually need a frame around it. Also, the set of pictures that make up your story need to be laid out effectively on the page – this is called the layout of the pictures.

▲ Frames
Look at existing comics to decide on a page size, before you plan your frames.

THE BOX STYLE

Remember that cartoons are read in the same way as a regular book, from left to right, starting at the top of the page. Choose the style of frame to suit your cartoon picture style.

▲ Frames
A loose, broken line.

▲ Frames
A hand drawn line.

▲ Frames
A line drawn with a ruler.

▲ Frames
A line with a drop shadow.

All of your frames
don't have to be the
same size. A big scene
can be effective.

YOUR
BLANK
PAGE

Lots of narrow, quick scenes can be shown by drawing smaller boxes close together.

Use a compass to draw a round scene and to curve the edges of the adjacent boxes.

PLANNING THE PAGE

Before you do any artwork, plan out each page as a simple doodle. Work out how many rows of pictures you can fit on, and where to put the title. Your final layout will also depend on what happens in the story!

If your pictures are varying shapes, make sure it is obvious which one the reader looks at next.

▼ Action comics
Pictures are really dynamic if things break out of the frame edge. Use "flash" or jagged frames for scenes such as battles.

The Story so Far

SO WHAT IS YOUR CARTOON CHARACTER GOING TO DO? YOU HAVE BUILT up its personality and lifestyle, and what it can and can't do. All you need now is a plot, whether it's a dramatic story, or just a brilliant joke that can be told in pictures.

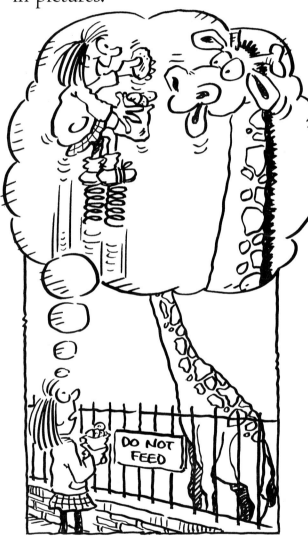

▲ Ideas
A simple idea is often best. Otherwise the reader can get confused about what is happening or who is who.

KEEPING THE READER INTERESTED The

Think of the reaction you want your readers to have. Do you want them to laugh or be sad, or possibly a bit of both? Whichever way, you need to keep the humor, action, and suspense, going until the end. That way your readers will keep on reading to find out what happens. Make them laugh or cry but make them wait!

▼ Thinking about it
As the comic strip is basically a picture story, try to think visually. Look out for comic situations that occur at home or school.

▲ Laughing
Make them roar with laughter.

▲ Crying
Bring tears to their eyes.

▲ Scared
Make their hair stand on end.

STORYLINE

The best way to plan your storyline is visually, as a cript (below), in which you can show the words and action separately. If you have an idea but keep getting stuck, make a "what if..." sheet and write down all the things that could happen, even the weirdest.

▼ Suspense
Keep them guessing until the very end.

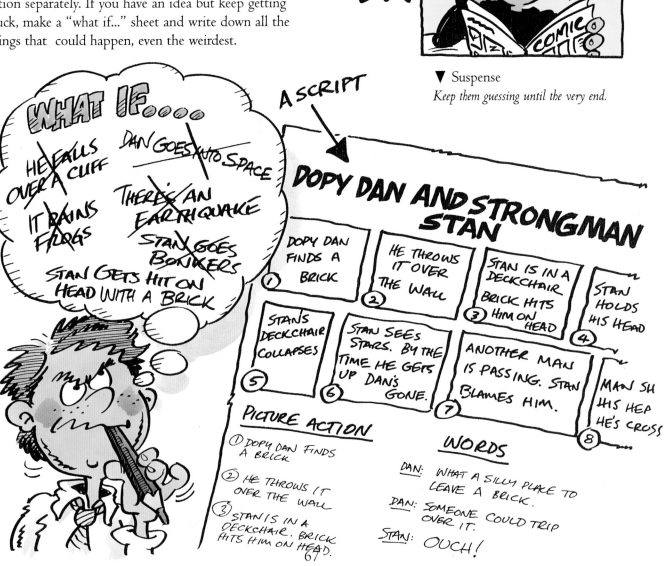

Storyboards

 YOU ARE FINALLY READY to start planning your actual cartoon strip. You do this by drawing a storyboard. This is a set of rough pictures which tell your story. Don't do them in too much detail to start with as you may want to make changes as you go.

▲ The storyboard
Your finished storyboard should have a series of finished pencil sketches and text in sequence. Show it to friends in case they suggest any changes before final artwork.

▼ Wallace and Grommit storyboards
On this spread are the storyboards of a famous animator, called Nick Park. They show how to create and work on a storyboard.

MAN RUNS TO DIVING BOARD

MAN PREPARES TO DIVE

MAN DIVES

OH DEAR! SOMEONE'S PULLED THE PLUG OUT

MAN SEES NO WATER

MAN CRASHES THROUGH FLOOR

How to make your Storyboard

Start by doing a rough sketch, then trace this neatly onto tracing paper, making any corrections as you go. Tack the separate frames lightly onto a board, and alter or add to the order until you are happy with everything. Then stick the pictures down, and you are ready to do the artwork.

The artwork

ON'T BE TEMPTED TO RUSH YOUR
final drawing. It does not have to be
completed all in one go, although it is a
good idea to work on it as often as you can, so
that you don't loose track of how you are doing.
Once your storyboard drawings are exactly right,
you need to copy them onto your artwork paper
or board.

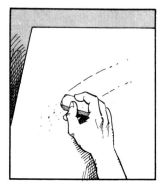

▲ Preparing the board
*The surface of the board can be
cleaned with an eraser to
remove any greasy spots.*

THE DRAWINGS

You may have to carefully copy all
your drawings from your storyboard
onto your artwork material. Or,
tape the storyboard to the window,
overlay thin artwork paper and
trace the whole strip in pencil.
Professionals use a lightbox.

▲ Using pencils
*Planning in pencil first allows
you to make last minute
changes and correct spelling.*

▼ Scaling
*Draw a grid over a drawing that is too big
or too small. Then draw another grid to the
correct size and copy square by square.*

▲ Protective coverings
*Always cover your artwork.
Think how you would feel if all
your hard work was ruined by tea!*

Adding Color

Next ink in (or use a fine felt pen) the whole strip, including all the words. Do the frame edges first, then the bubbles, words, and finally the pictures. Now you are ready to color in. It's a good idea to do one color at a time, that way it will be consistent throughout the strip. Your character should look the same in the last frame as in the first. If you make a mistake, cut out that frame or glue on a clean patch.

▲ Overlays
You can use overlays over your base artwork to add speech bubbles or another character.

WHAT YOU NEED
Artwork paper or board
Glue or sticky tape
Pencils, ruler, eraser
Compass or round plate
Pens, crayons, paints, inks
layout paper

The end

Y̲OUR ARTWORK IS finished! Read through the story to check for any mistakes, and tidy up the artwork by erasing any pencil lines and clean up messy frame edges.

◀ Overlays
Professionals write the words on a tracing paper overlay. This is so that if their cartoon is published in another country, a different overlay can be easily done in another language.

Correction fluid can be used to white out a spelling mistake. Then draw over it.

LOOK AFTER YOUR ARTWORK

Artwork is easily damaged so protect it once it is finished. Tape it onto some card and put a cover on it, made from acetate or colored paper.

It's a good idea, before you show off your strip cartoon to your friends, to make a copy of it. Accidents can happen! Take it into a copy shop, and get a photocopy of it. If you can get a color copy done (but this is somewhat expensive) then you can show the color copy to your friends and keep the artwork safe.

▶ Display your artwork up
You can hang your finished cartoon strip up on a wall at home, or in your school. It is best not to hang artwork up in direct sunlight as some colors will fade. Felt tip pens and some inks fade quickest, while watercolors and colored crayons will last longer.

Original artwork also makes great presents, if you can bear to give all that hardwork away.

► Branch out!

If your family and friends like your cartoon character, you don't have to stick to cartoon strips. You can branch out into badges or stickers, or make up some puzzles or games featuring your favorite character. Ask your art teacher at school for helpful hints on how to get things printed, or if this is too expensive, you can make your own. T-shirts are fun to make, using a plain white shirt and special crayons for drawing on material.

◄ Expand your ideas

If your first cartoon strip was successful, or more importantly, if you enjoyed doing it, why not try to follow it up with a few more?

You have learnt where and how to seek inspiration for good ideas, so make it a habit to constantly keep your eyes and ears open for other cartoons. You will probably find that the more you draw the more ideas will come to you, and the quicker and easier it will become to bring them to life. If you lose interest in an idea though, it is best to leave it because if it starts to bore you it will certainly bore the people you show it to!

► Distribution!

If you do a number of cartoon strips, staple copies of then together to make a complete comic. You can design a cover for it as well, and see your name "in print." Who knows where it will end.

...Or the beginning

Aing CARTOON ANIMATION IS ALMOST the same as a cartoon strip, except that the characters really move and really speak. In animation you still have a scene, which then cuts to another, just like looking at a strip cartoon from frame to frame. Try simple animation by making a flick book, or a zoetrope, to start.

EARLY ANIMATION

At the turn of the twentieth-century comic strips and magazines were popular. This coincided with the development of animation. Some comic characters were brought to life in the early animations, and then many more were invented especially for animation. Some of the these were then turned into comic strip characters as well.

Dino Dinosaur
A panel from Winsor McCay's only known comic strip of the character Dino the Dinosaur, *drawn in 1909. Even in this small example, McCay's ability to suggest scale is apparent.*

▲ Animated characters
Comic cartoon characters were perfect for animation because they were simple. This made it easier to do the thousands of drawings needed to make them move even one step.

MODERN ANIMATION

There are special techniques today to create the cartoon animation you see at the movies or on television. The artwork is separated into backgrounds done on paper, and the moving objects or characters are painted onto clear acetate (plastic sheets) called "cells." The cells are placed over the background and filmed one by one, using a special camera called a "rostrum camera."

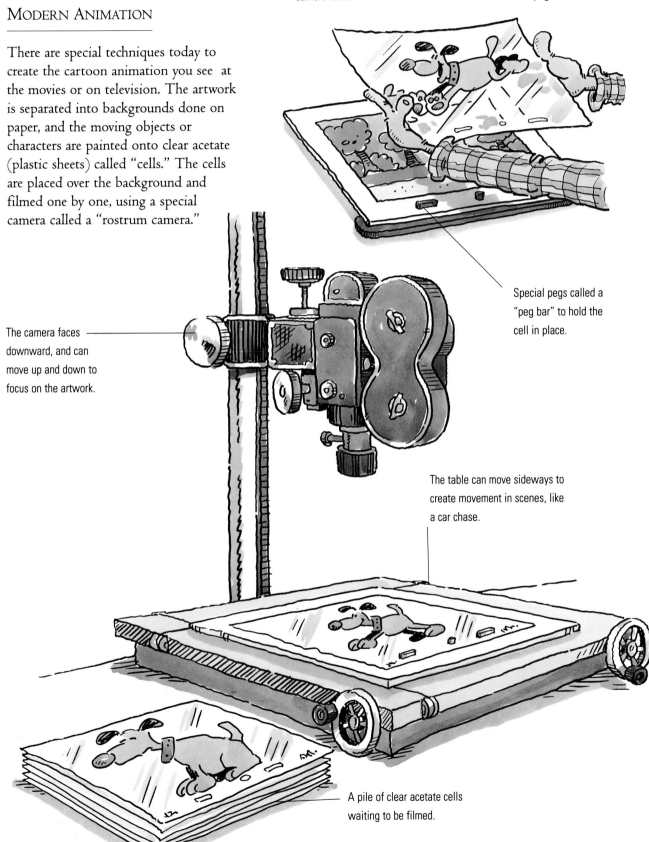

The background painted onto paper, and placed onto the camera table.

An acetate cell being placed over the background. Note the holes for the "peg bar".

Special pegs called a "peg bar" to hold the cell in place.

The camera faces downward, and can move up and down to focus on the artwork.

The table can move sideways to create movement in scenes, like a car chase.

A pile of clear acetate cells waiting to be filmed.

Back to the drawing board

PLANNING ANIMATION IS VERY SIMILAR to planning a strip cartoon. First you need your character, story, and script – but you can use ones you have already created – and then these need to be made into an animation storyboard, which is slightly different to a comic strip storyboard.

1 DOG WALKS ALONG STREET
SOUNDS OF BIRDS SINGING. CUT TO:....

2 SUNSHINE AND BIRDS SINGING.
"HOW MUCH IS THAT DOGGIE IN THE WINDOW?".....

3 DOG STOPS AND LOOKS UP. THEN SAYS:
"THAT TUNE SOUNDS FAMILIAR."

4 CUT TO

5 TURNS TO CAMERA AND SAYS:
"IT'S THAT PESKY BIRD BRAIN. REMEMBER LAST NIGHT!"

6 MIX TO: KENNEL AT NIGHT.
BIRD BRAIN IS PECKING AWAY AT THE WOOD.
S.F.X: PECKING SOUNDS.

7 CUT TO: INSIDE OF DOG KENNEL. DOG WITH PAWS OVER EARS.

8

The frames need to be separate from the text, and all the same size and shape.

The text is written as action and dialog.

CREATING THE STORYBOARD

An animation storyboard is a series of finished sketches and frames, with text underneath to explain the action and showing the dialog. Unlike a comic strip storyboard, each frame needs to be the same size and shape, and there are no speech bubbles.

▶ Using a video
If you have access to a home video camera you can video the storyboard frame by frame to see how well it works.

Discussing the Storyboard

When your storyboard is finished it is a good idea to show it to friends or family — or anyone whose opinion you value — and see what they think.

Criticism is always hard to take, but it may be constructive. Or they may come up with many other ideas for cartoons, and ways to make your storyline even better than it is already.

MAN RUNS TO DIVING BOARD MAN PREPARES TO DIVE MAN DIVES

OH DEAR! SOMEONE'S PULLED THE PLUG OUT MAN SEES NO WATER MAN CRASHES THROUGH FLOOR

Sounds

Sounds are almost as important as pictures in animation. Your character will need a distinctive voice, as the way it sounds may be remembered as much as how it looks.

You may want to invent a catchphrase, or a special way that it talks and sings. Experiment with various voices yourself and record them onto a cassette.

▼ Different voices
Tape your pets for animal noises, or ask your friends to play different parts.

HOW DO I SOUND?

MORE LIKE A CAT THAN A DOG.

MAYBE I SHOULD STICK TO BARKING!

CLIP CLOP CLIP CLOP

◀ Sound effects
Think of ways to create sound effects for your story. There are standard ones, such as using coconut shells for horses hooves, and crumpling paper for rustling leaves. Experiment for yourself with everyday household things.

77

Making it move!

WHEN YOU WATCH A CARTOON movie, the projector makes 24 frames of film hit the screen every second, one after another. But you should do one drawing for every two frames, as the eye will see this as continuous movement when it is projected.

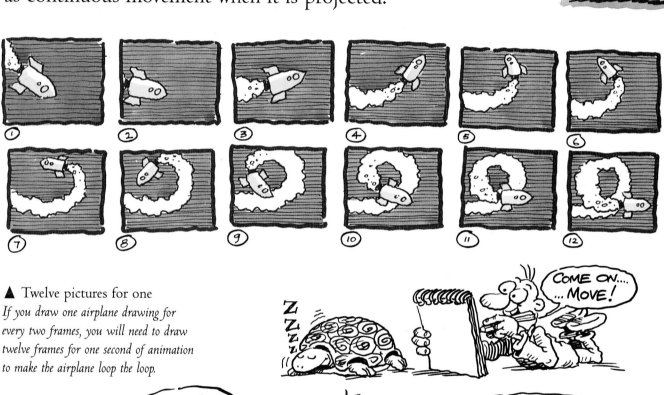

▲ Twelve pictures for one
If you draw one airplane drawing for every two frames, you will need to draw twelve frames for one second of animation to make the airplane loop the loop.

COME ON....
... MOVE!

O.K. NOW WALK!

HE'LL WANT ME TO FLY NEXT!!

▲ Look and learn.
The best way to animate is to look carefully at movement, especially slowly in a mirror.

Muybridge.
Muybridge (1830-1904)
began to study animal
locomotion in 1887. He
then moved onto human
movement. He took these
pictures by setting up a row
of cameras, which shot in
sequence one after the other. So
each frame in this picture was
taken by a separate camera.

► Key drawings

Try to draw the main positions of the movement you want to animate, especially the beginning, middle, and end. These are called "key drawings." The number of drawings you do depends on how complicated the movement is. For something simple, like picking up a mug (left), three would be enough.

Start position
The man is just about to
pick the mug up.

Midway
He raises the mug
midway to his mouth.

End position
He reaches his mouth
and has a drink.

MOVEMENT

You can work out movement using stick people. Just do a series of small drawings of a stick figure walking, running, kicking a football, or jumping (see below). Then run your eye along them one by one and actually see how the animation would work. If you blink between each frame, your eye acts just like a camera.

▼ Picture sequences.
Run your eye along the series of pictures on the bottom of this spread. You will see it does look as though he is running, kicking the ball, slipping, and then falling over.

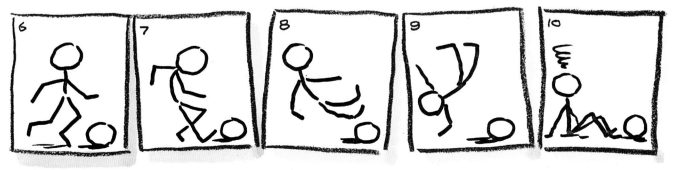

The "inbetweens"

ANIMATION IS BASICALLY DOING A NUMBER of character drawings in "key positions," and then doing the drawings inbetween. This is called "inbetweening." The number of inbetween drawings, called "inbetweens," and "key drawings" will depend on how long you want the movement to last.

◄ Key drawings
Here are three key drawings for turning a head, which is slightly more complicated than lifting a cup. This is because the whole face moves as well. Number them, and do them on tracing paper.

► Start with the eyes
It is easiest to start with the eyes. Your new "inbetween" eye goes midway between the eyes labeled one and two.

NEW POSITION
① ②

▲ Overlapping
Place drawing two over one, so that you can see both heads. Then put tracing paper over both, and draw a head inbetween them.

▼ Inbetweens
Keep doing drawings inbetween the key drawings, and re-number them all carefully. If you want a head to turn more slowly you can do extra inbetweens.

IN BETWEENS

Start position with one inbetween before the mid-position.

End position with one inbetween after the mid-position.

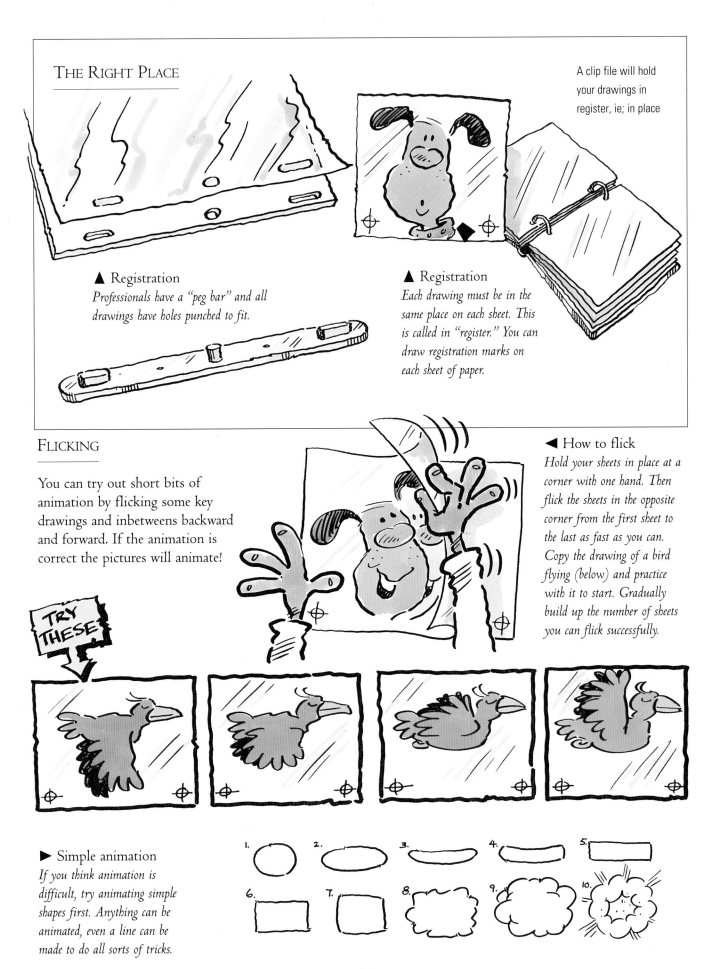

THE RIGHT PLACE

A clip file will hold your drawings in register, ie; in place

▲ Registration
Professionals have a "peg bar" and all drawings have holes punched to fit.

▲ Registration
Each drawing must be in the same place on each sheet. This is called in "register." You can draw registration marks on each sheet of paper.

FLICKING

You can try out short bits of animation by flicking some key drawings and inbetweens backward and forward. If the animation is correct the pictures will animate!

TRY THESE

◀ How to flick
Hold your sheets in place at a corner with one hand. Then flick the sheets in the opposite corner from the first sheet to the last as fast as you can. Copy the drawing of a bird flying (below) and practice with it to start. Gradually build up the number of sheets you can flick successfully.

▶ Simple animation
If you think animation is difficult, try animating simple shapes first. Anything can be animated, even a line can be made to do all sorts of tricks.

1. 2. 3. 4. 5.
6. 7. 8. 9. 10.

Shortcuts

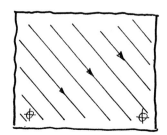

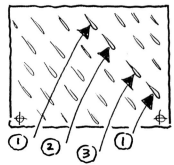

I F YOU LOOK AT THINGS THAT MOVE, YOU'LL notice that many actions are made up of a set of movements that are repeated. Look at a side view of someone walking – once they have put one leg forward and then the other, the rest is a repeat of the same action. Animators call this a "cycle" of action.

CYCLES

"Cycles" really help animators, as only one set of movements needs to be drawn, and these can be filmed over and over again. Any movement in which there is a pattern can become a cycle, but not random action.

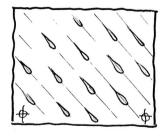

▼ **Butterfly flying cycle**
Here is a cycle of butterfly wings, in six steps. The cycle of action goes from steps one to six, and then back to one again, and so on.

▲Raining overlays
Draw the direction of the rain on overlay one; draw some rain on overlay two; draw more rain farther down on overlay three.

▼ **Simple walking cyle**
This is a simple walk cycle. Notice that the arms, head, and the rest of the body all move as well as the legs. A more realistic walk cycle would need 16 cycles.

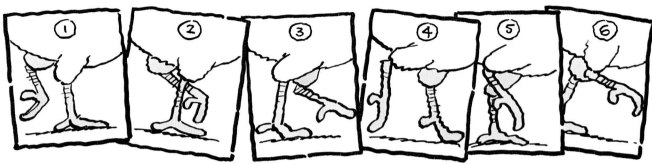

▲ Chicken walk

Chicken legs are a good way to practice walk cycles. Do each leg in a different color so you know which is which. With all action cycles draw your key positions and then as many inbetweens as you want.

► Waving

An arm wave is drawn as a cycle moving from bottom to top, then top to bottom. You would film from one to five, five to one, then start again.

Work out a walk cycle in stick legs first. As with the chicken legs draw different colored legs.

Backgrounds

IN ANIMATION THE characters and the backgrounds need to be separate pieces of artwork, so that the position of the character can be seen over the same background scene. Although the background is a separate piece of artwork, it should still relate to the characters and action, so they work as a whole.

▲ Character and background work together
Both the background and the character show that it is a windy day. They fit together so well that you can't guess they were separate.

SLOTTING TOGETHER

You can place more than one "cell" on the background artwork, so that different characters and objects can be included to add variety to the background, and to give the impression of movement.

A background

An acetate cell with the character painted on

Another cell with a different animation on

Backgrounds and both cells put together

▶ Panning backgrounds
When you see a chase in an animated movie or program, the characters really look as though they are running. In fact they are animated as if they are running on the spot. Behind them a long scene called a panning background is moved to create the impression of speed.

► A city scene
You can add extra interest to a city scene by painting different vehicles and pedestrians on separate acetate cells and varying them.

▲ A country scene
A country scene may look slightly bare with only open fields. So add different animals, farmers, or a tractor to the scene. They do not have to stay in the far background; this horse could gallop right up to the gate fo added impact.

Flick books

BECAUSE ANIMATION IS EXPENSIVE TO GET onto film or video, you can only practice bits of it for now. Making a flick book will give you a chance to see your pictures move. You can either buy some small plain paper pads, or make your own. Try something short and easy at first in pencil, so that you can correct any little details that don't work.

MAKING A FLICKBOOK

1 *Use fairly stiff paper and cut it up into small rectangles. Any size will do but small ones are easier to flick. Cut 25 to 30 pieces.*

2 *Do the animation drawings on each piece. Number each one on the back in case they get muddled up. Keep it fairly simple. It is best not to bother with a background as you will have to copy it onto every page.*

3 *The cartoon must be in the same place on each page for them to animate properly. Leave a space on the left hand side for your glue or staples. To work out the animation, either start on the first piece of paper and change the picture as you go along or draw a "master" drawing with the different positions marked on it. You can trace these off using carbon paper or rub pencil on the back.*

Actual size for you to trace off.

4 *Write your title on the first page and then arrange them in the right order. Staple or glue each sheet together. Use sticky tape to tape over the spine. This will keep your pages neatly together.*

5 *To see your animation come to life, hold the book in your left hand and flick with your right. You may need to practice this a few times until you get it absolutely right.*

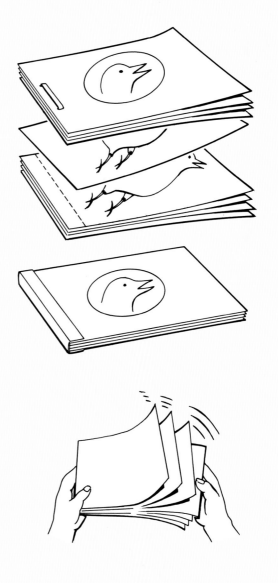

Zoetrope

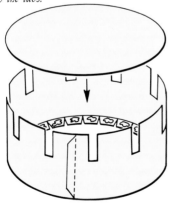

The zoetrope was a Victorian toy in which strips of pictures were put, then viewed through slits as the zoetrope was spun around. The slits act like a movie projector. Each one shows the eye one picture at a time very quickly so that they become animated.

HOW TO MAKE A ZOETROPE

1 *Draw a circle on the card with a compass, and cut it out. Make a cross slit in the center as shown. If you use a plate, measure the distance round the edge to work out how long to make the wall.*

2 *Take your card and draw and cut out the wall, making ten evenly spaced slits. These should be about 5mm (1/4 inch) wide. Make it in sections if your card isn't long enough. Cut out tab shapes at the bottom and on one edge of the wall, as shown in the diagram.*

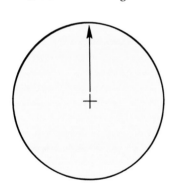

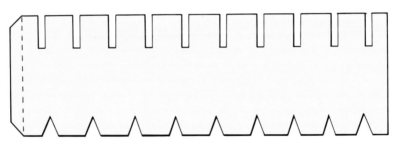

3 *Bend the tabs inwards and drop in the base to make sure it is the right size. If it is too big, trim it to size. Put some glue on the upper surfaces of the tabs. Then, glue the wall to make a cylinder. Drop the base down into the cylinder again and this time glue it to the tabs.*

The next stage is making the animation. Here are some examples of the kind of drawings you could do.

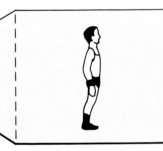

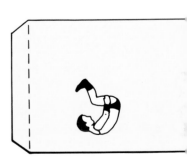

88

MAKING THE ANIMATION

Because a zoetrope is round, and the strip of pictures will be viewed continuously, they must show an animation "cycle" – an animation that keeps on repeating itself without any gaps.

You can make as many animations as you like, but do one first to check it's the right size.

Keep your image fairly simple to begin with.

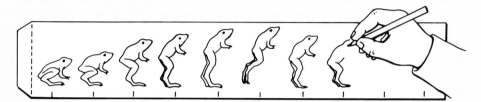

▼ Cylinder
Cut a strip of paper the same length as the wall but only half as high. Put ten marks spaced the same distance apart as the wall slits. Draw an image above each mark.

▼ Fixing together.
Before you stick both ends of your strip together, check that it fits neatly into your zoetrope. Push a pencil through the slit.

▼ Using the zoetrope.
Turn the pencil to spin the zoetrope and look through the slits. It needs to be well balanced to turn evenly.

Glossary

Bleed
The colors made from paints, inks, or chunky felt pens will run, or merge together, when wet or used on wet paper. This is known as bleeding.

Carbon Paper
A thin sheet of paper coated on one side with a dark waxy substance. When you write or draw on the uncoated side, the substance is transferred onto a sheet of paper underneath the carbon paper, and makes a copy of the writing or drawing.

Color photocopy
A color reproduction of any image made using a color photocopier. The photocopy uses four colors (black, blue, yellow, magenta) to recreate all the colors in the image. It does not give an exact color reproduction but it is a fair representation.

Cross hatching
A series of lines drawn overlapping themselves to create areas of shading, density, and solidity in a drawing.

Layout paper
This is a thin paper with a smooth surface, similar to typo paper. It is white and semi-transparent and takes most types of mediums, but it is too thin for paints and will wrinkle up.

Watercolor paper
This is a thick white, or creamy-white, paper. It is very absorbent and its surface has a slight texture. It is generally used with watercolor paints or inks.

Pencil rub
This is similar to carbon paper, only you can make it yourself. Rub a soft pencil onto the back of a sheet of paper. Place this side face downwards onto a clean sheet of paper below. Draw the outline of the picture you want to copy on the clean side of the top copy. This will transfer the image onto the copy paper below.

Index

Photo credits

Quarto Children's Books Limited would like to thank the following for for providing photographs,
and for granting permission to reproduce copyright material.

(a = above, b = below, c = centre, l = left, r = right)

British Museum: p10b. British Film Institute: p90ar. Paul Johnson: p10ar, p44ar.
Edward Muybridge Collection, Kingston Museum & Heritage Service: p79al. James Puttnam: p11c.
Mansell Colection: p11al. Quarto: p16bc, p16br Chas Wilder p12ar.

While every effort has been made to trace and acknowledge all copyright holders,
we would like to apologise should any omissions have been made.